CIVIL WAR
TECHNOLOGY

BY TAMMY GAGNE

CONTENT CONSULTANT
Charles D. Ross
Professor of Physics
Longwood University

Core Library

An Imprint of Abdo Publishing
abdopublishing.com

Cover image: Union troops stand beside large mortars
near Yorktown, Virginia, in 1862.

abdopublishing.com

Published by Abdo Publishing, a division of ABDO, PO Box 398166,
Minneapolis, Minnesota 55439. Copyright © 2018 by Abdo Consulting
Group, Inc. International copyrights reserved in all countries. No part of this
book may be reproduced in any form without written permission from the
publisher. Core Library™ is a trademark and logo of Abdo Publishing.

Printed in the United States of America, North Mankato, Minnesota
042017
092017

THIS BOOK CONTAINS
RECYCLED MATERIALS

Cover Photo: Library of Congress
Interior Photos: Library of Congress, 1, 6–7, 45; National Archives, 4–5; Library of Congress/
Archive Photos/Getty Images, 12–13; PhotoQuest/Archive Photos/Getty Images, 16; Shutterstock
Images, 17; Stock Montage/Archive Photos/Getty Images, 18–19; Buyenlarge/Archive Photos/
Getty Images, 21, 34–35; Science & Society Picture Library/Getty Images, 24; MPI/Archive Photos/
Getty Images, 26–27; John Parrot/Stocktrek Images/Getty Images, 29; Interim Archives/Archive
Photos/Getty Images, 30–31; David Knox/Hulton Archive/Getty Images, 37; Red Line Editorial, 38

Editor: Arnold Ringstad
Imprint Designer: Maggie Villaume
Series Design Direction: Nikki Farinella

Publisher's Cataloging-in-Publication Data

Names: Gagne, Tammy, author.
Title: Civil War technology / by Tammy Gagne.
Description: Minneapolis, MN : Abdo Publishing, 2018. | Series: War technology |
    Includes bibliographical references and index.
Identifiers: LCCN 2017930456 | ISBN 9781532111891 (lib. bdg.) |
    ISBN 9781680789744 (ebook)
Subjects: LCSH: United States--History--Civil War, 1861-1865--Technology--
    Juvenile literature. | Technology--United States--19th century--Juvenile
    literature.
Classification: DDC 973.7/8--dc23
    LC record available at http://lccn.loc.gov/2017930456

CONTENTS

A NATION
DIVIDED

It was the spring of 1862. The CSS *Virginia* left Norfolk, Virginia. It searched for Union ships just a few miles off the coastline. The *Virginia* looked unlike other ships of the American Civil War (1861–1865). Its angular iron sides rose above the water. Ten cannons poked out from its thick armor.

Confederate officer Franklin Buchanan steamed the *Virginia* toward the USS *Cumberland*. The wooden Union ship was no match for the Confederate ironclad. The *Virginia* had a 1,500-pound (680-kg) battering ram. It smashed through the

The *Virginia*, *right*, looked vastly different from earlier ships.

The *Monitor, right,* was able to put up a fight against the *Virginia.*

Cumberland's sides. The ship began to take on water. The *Virginia* got tangled up in the wreckage, and it looked as though both ships might go down. But then the iron ram broke off. The *Virginia* escaped.

Buchanan next set his sights on the USS *Congress.* The *Congress* attempted to escape. But the Southern

sailors fired upon it. It seemed the *Congress* would
surrender. Buchanan appeared on the deck of the
Virginia. Just then, a musket ball fired from the *Congress*
struck him. The *Virginia* retreated. The end of the battle
would have to wait until the next day.

IRONCLAD SHIPS

The North had a major naval advantage. The South did not have its own navy at the start of the war. It did not try to match the Union's navy. Instead it focused on defending its harbors. Ironclad ships were one way to do this. The first battle between ironclads was between the *Virginia* and the *Monitor*. Neither side won the battle. Still, it marked the beginning of a new way to fight on water.

A new day brought a new Confederate commander. The *Virginia*'s Catesby Jones continued the fight. He attacked the USS *Minnesota*. But this time, the Union was ready. The USS *Monitor* joined the *Minnesota*. Like the *Virginia*, the *Monitor* was an ironclad ship. Rather than angled sides, it had a mostly flat top. Only a circular turret with a pair of cannons rose above the water.

The ironclads traded cannon fire for hours. Most shots simply dented their thick armor. The battle ended in a draw. Both ships finally retreated. It would go down in history as the first-ever battle between ironclad ships.

The *Virginia* and the *Monitor* became famous examples of Civil War technology.

POLITICS AND WEAPONS

By 1860 the issue of slavery had deeply divided the United States. Northern states had outlawed the practice. They did not want it spreading to new states. Southern states still enslaved people. Eleven Southern states decided to secede to keep slavery. They called themselves the Confederate States of America. The Northern states were known as the Union. They did not accept the South's secession. Led by President Abraham Lincoln, the Union went to war to

PERSPECTIVES
A NORTHERN ADVANTAGE

Many technologies became available during the Civil War. The Confederacy often did not have the same access to them that the Union did. Most weapons factories were located in the North. The Union also had more railroad lines. This made it easier to transport high-tech weapons to the front lines.

reunite the country. The war would also bring about the end of US slavery.

The Civil War was a time of great change. The war ripped apart the nation politically. The struggle over slavery led to massive social change. In addition, the war resulted in incredible technological development. It broke out in the middle of the Industrial Revolution. In this period, machines and factories were changing the way societies worked. Many of the war's officers had been studying the latest science. Their influence moved military technology forward. Advanced technology helped the Union win the war.

STRAIGHT TO THE
SOURCE

Historian James McPherson noted in an interview that Abraham Lincoln was passionate about technology. Lincoln even tested new weapons personally on the White House lawn:

> *I think he may also have tested one or more versions of the Sharps single-shot breach-loading rifle. He also tested the 'coffee-mill gun'—an early version of a hand-cranked machine gun. He watched the testing of big naval guns at the navy yard on the Anacostia River and developed a close friendship with John Dahlgren, head of the navy yard (later an admiral) and a weapons expert. When Lincoln went to West Point in June 1862 to consult with Winfield Scott, he also went a little farther up the Hudson to the Cold Spring Armory to watch the testing of Parrott rifled artillery.*

Source: Henry J. Reske. "Abraham Lincoln: A Technology Leader of His Time." *US News & World Report*. US News & World Report, February 11, 2009. Web. Accessed January 30, 2017.

Back It Up

McPherson is using evidence to support his point. Write a sentence describing his point. Then write down two pieces of evidence he uses to support his point.

FIREARMS: SHOOTING FASTER AND FARTHER

Firearms technology had been improving in the years before the Civil War. The most common guns in previous wars had been smoothbore muskets. These long guns had smooth barrels. They took several seconds to load and fire. They were inaccurate. A target had to be within about 100 yards (91 m). Some soldiers still used muskets in the Civil War. However, advancing technology offered several better options.

Personal firearms were the most common weapons of the Civil War.

RIFLES AND MINIÉ BALLS

Rifles had a better range than muskets. The inside of a rifle's barrel is not smooth. Instead, it has spiraling grooves. These grooves spin the bullet as it leaves the gun. Just as with throwing a football, spinning helps the bullet fly straighter and farther. Early rifles had three times the range of a smoothbore musket.

In 1849 French officer Claude-Étienne Minié invented new ammunition. It improved range even more. His bullets were known as Minié balls. They had hollow bases

BREECHLOADERS

Before the Civil War, muskets were muzzle-loaded weapons. This meant the user placed the ammunition into the gun from the mouth of its barrel. Newer breech-loading weapons made the process easier. Users inserted ammunition into these guns from the back of the barrel. Early versions of breechloaders had to be reloaded before each shot. In time, however, engineers developed repeating breech-loading weapons. They included the Henry rifle. It could fire 16 shots before the user had to reload.

that expanded upon firing. They could reach a target 880 yards (805 m) away.

Many officers had their troops continue to fight in tight rows. This had worked well in earlier wars, when muskets were inaccurate. But now it resulted in extremely high casualties.

PERSPECTIVES

WEAPONS PRODUCTION

During the war, the North had a major industrial advantage. It was able to greatly increase production of both guns and ammunition. In an effort to catch up, Confederate soldiers captured equipment from the US Armory at Harpers Ferry, Virginia, in 1861. They used it to create their own weapons factories.

A soldier using a regular rifle had to reload his weapon for each shot. The repeating rifle saved time. Firing the weapon loaded the next round automatically. A repeating rifle could be fired over and over again. This new type of weapon was in use by 1863. It was mostly used by cavalry troops. The most popular model

Gatling patented his design in 1862.

was the Spencer carbine. It could fire seven shots in 30 seconds.

GATLING GUNS

American inventor Richard Gatling wanted to reduce the number of soldiers being sent off to war. His solution was to design a gun that could fire many bullets quickly. He hoped such a powerful weapon would discourage wars. His design became popular. But the invention did not reduce the number of soldiers fighting in wars.

FIRING RATE

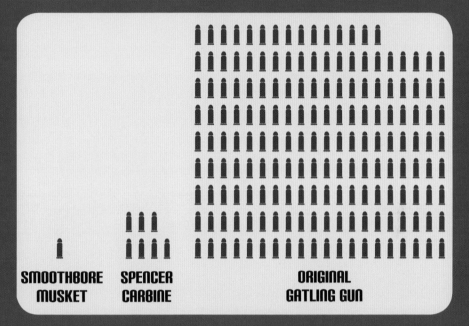

SMOOTHBORE MUSKET

SPENCER CARBINE

ORIGINAL GATLING GUN

This graphic shows how many rounds three Civil War weapons could fire in 30 seconds. What advantages would a faster firing rate give to a soldier? Are there any disadvantages to giving a soldier the opportunity to fire large numbers of bullets?

The original Gatling gun had six barrels. A hand crank rotated the barrels around a central shaft. New bullets were fed into the barrels automatically. The weapon could fire 350 rounds in just one minute. Gatling upgraded the gun to include ten barrels. The new version could fire 400 rounds per minute. His gun was used during the Union's siege of Petersburg, Virginia, from 1864 to 1865.

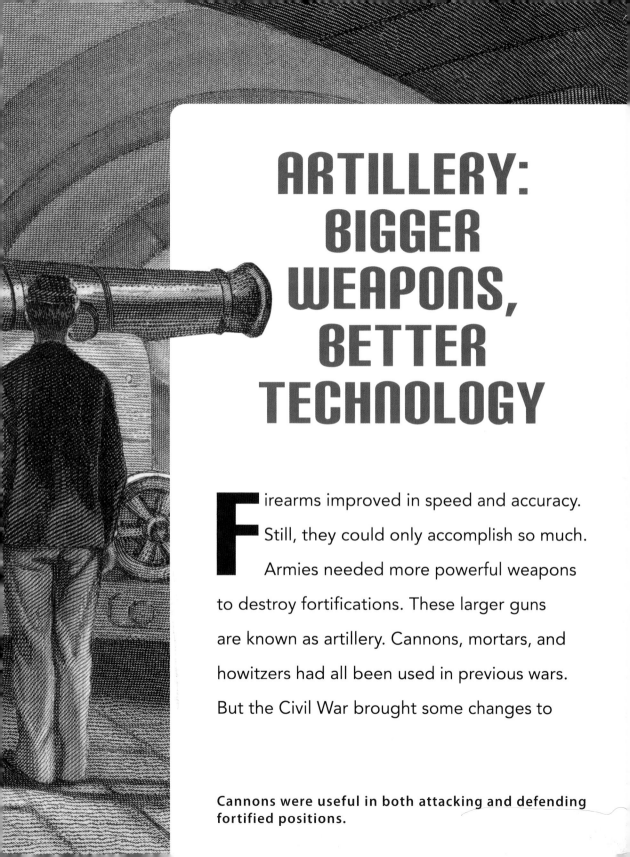

ARTILLERY: BIGGER WEAPONS, BETTER TECHNOLOGY

Firearms improved in speed and accuracy. Still, they could only accomplish so much. Armies needed more powerful weapons to destroy fortifications. These larger guns are known as artillery. Cannons, mortars, and howitzers had all been used in previous wars. But the Civil War brought some changes to

Cannons were useful in both attacking and defending fortified positions.

these big guns. It even included the early use of a new weapon: the rocket launcher.

CANNONS

Civil War cannons included the 6-pounder gun and the 12-pounder gun. The 10- and 20-pounder versions of the Parrott rifle were also used. These weapons were named for the approximate weight of the shot they fired. Cannons could inflict significant damage to the enemy.

Just as with handheld firearms, rifling improved cannons. Rifled guns could fire farther than smooth-barreled cannons. They also had a better chance of hitting their targets.

During the Civil War, cannon manufacturers started using iron instead of bronze. Iron was plentiful in the Northern states. This made it an ideal building material for the Union. As a side benefit, iron was slightly lighter than bronze.

In an age before motor vehicles, horses were used to pull Parrott rifles and other cannons.

MORTARS

Civil War mortars were shorter and thicker than cannons. They fired heavy explosive projectiles in a high arc. Exploding fragments fell on the enemy from above. The explosions would also cause wooden targets to ignite. This caused even more damage.

SUPPORTING THE UNION THROUGH TECHNOLOGY

Robert Parker Parrott taught physics in the 1820s. He then became a captain in the US Army. In the late 1830s, he left the military to become the superintendent of a foundry. During this time, he experimented with cannon designs. Many iron cannons were shattering when fired. Parrott solved the problem. He placed a wrought-iron hoop around his cannon's barrel. The hoop made the barrel stronger. In 1861 he patented this technology. Parrott was a supporter of the Union. He offered to make these cannons for the Union at cost. This meant that he charged only the amount of money it cost him to make the weapons. He did not sell them for a profit.

The best-known mortar of the Civil War was called the Dictator. It weighed in at 17,000 pounds (7,700 kg). It could deliver a huge blow to the enemy. The Dictator could launch a 200-pound (91-kg) shell about 2.5 miles (4 km). This weapon was used in the Union siege of Petersburg.

HOWITZERS

A howitzer could not fire as far as a cannon. Like mortars, howitzers launched shots at higher elevations.

Howitzers were also lighter than the other big guns. This made them easier for soldiers to move around.

Most howitzers were smoothbore weapons. However, rifled models became more popular during the war. The most common Civil War howitzer was the 1841 12-pounder. This weapon could fire a shell more than 1,000 yards (914 m).

ROCKET LAUNCHERS

The Union used a weapon called the Hale rocket launcher.

TOO GOOD TO BE TRUE?

One of the most mysterious Civil War weapons was the Confederacy's Winans steam gun. This artillery weapon was invented by William Joslin and Charles Dickinson. Sitting on an armored train carriage, it used steam to fire its ammunition. According to newspapers, the weapon could fire 200 rounds per minute. It never saw action, however. Union soldiers decided to destroy the weapon after capturing it. No one knew for sure why they did this. Some people suspected it wasn't as effective as the rumors claimed.

Small fins on the back of the Hale rocket gave it a stabilizing spin.

It was a metal tube that fired spin-stabilized rockets. A spin-stabilized rocket rotates as it flies.

The Hale launcher fired 7-inch (18-cm) and 10-inch (25-cm) rockets up to 2,000 yards (1,829 m). This was impressive for the era, but the rockets were still difficult for soldiers to aim. During the war, most were used by the US Navy.

The Confederacy also dabbled in rocket launchers. They experimented with Congreve rockets. These weapons looked like large bottle rockets. The British had used Congreve rockets against the United States during the War of 1812 (1812–1815). Decades later, during the Civil War, Congreve rockets were still inaccurate. They did not receive much use.

FURTHER EVIDENCE

Chapter Three discusses artillery technology used during the Civil War. What is the main idea of this chapter? What key evidence supports this idea? Take a look at the website below. Find information from the site that supports the main idea of this chapter. Does the information support an existing piece of evidence in the chapter, or does it add new evidence?

CIVIL WAR ARTILLERY
abdocorelibrary.com/civil-war-tech

STRONGER SHIPS

Before the Civil War, ships were made almost entirely of wood. They depended on their sails for movement. Ships traded cannon shots until one sank. This basic strategy did not change. Still, the Civil War saw significant advances in military ships. Technology changed the materials used to build them. It also changed how they moved.

STEAMING AHEAD

Early steam-powered ships had been around before the 1800s. They had not been widely used in warfare. For centuries, sailing ships had made up the backbones of navies.

Steam power and iron armor played important roles in the Civil War's naval battles.

PERSPECTIVES
SECRET WEAPONS

Today torpedoes are self-propelled underwater missiles. But during the Civil War, the word *torpedo* referred to a stationary explosive device. These are now called mines. Such a weapon was especially effective for secret attacks. One type of torpedo was set in cast iron. It was then dipped in beeswax and pitch. It was covered in coal dust. The result looked like an ordinary piece of coal. Confederate spies would place coal torpedoes in Union coal supplies. When the torpedo was shoveled into a ship's steam engine, it would explode and damage the ship.

The problem with them was that they relied heavily on wind. The weather affected battles nearly as much as the weapons themselves.

Steam-powered ships burned coal to turn propellers. This gave navies more control over speed and direction. By the start of the Civil War, all new US Navy ships were powered by steam. These ships looked similar to the older

Most naval ships, including those with steam power, were still equipped with sails.

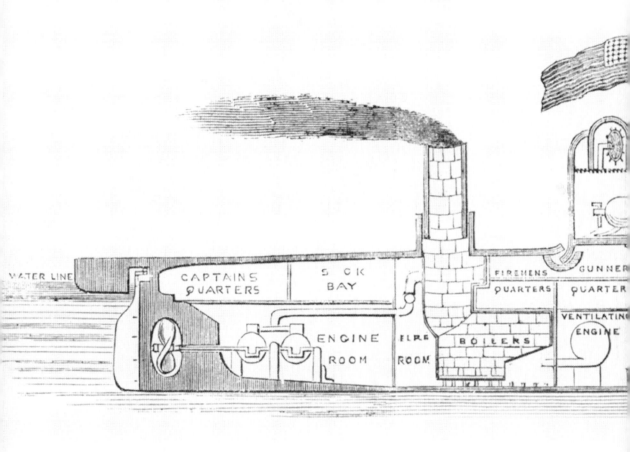

This cross section shows the typical layout of a Union ironclad ship.

ones. On most ships, the sails remained. Using sails saved fuel. The navy continued using them when speed wasn't important. People could tell the newer ships from the old ones by looking for the smokestacks.

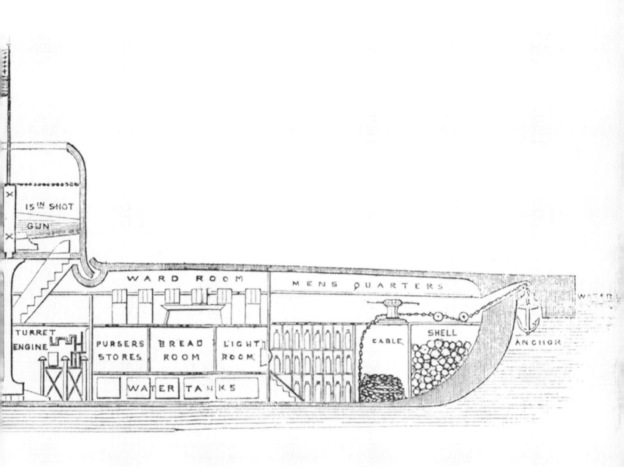

RISE OF THE IRONCLADS

Shipbuilders continued using wood for building vessels during the Civil War. But it became clear that wood had important weaknesses. Explosive cannon fire caused wooden ships to break apart and burn. This proved

THE *H. L. HUNLEY*

The first sinking of a naval ship by a submarine happened during the Civil War. The Confederate sub was called the *H. L. Hunley*. It was named after the engineer who designed it. Hunley and 12 other men had died during training exercises in the vessel. But Lieutenant George Dixon gave the sub another chance. In November 1863, Dixon and his crew attacked the *Housatonic*. They attached a bomb to the Union vessel. The secret mission sank the *Housatonic*. The sinking did not impact the war significantly. However, it marked an important shift in naval technology. The *H. L. Hunley* sank shortly after the attack. It was eventually found and raised to the surface in 2000.

costly in more ways than one. First, sailors died when ships went down. Second, it took a lot of time and money to build more vessels.

Engineers realized ships needed protection. They decided to try covering the wood with metal. This armor plating was usually iron or steel. When an artillery shell hit these materials, it dented them. But it did not penetrate the ship. Armor kept ships afloat and saved the lives of many sailors.

Ironclad ships were heavier than wooden ones. Sails could not move these ships as quickly. The steam engine helped solve this problem. Before heading into battle, crews lowered the sails and started the steam engines. Like wood, sails were quick to catch fire, so this step helped protect ships.

EXPLORE ONLINE

Chapter Four discusses naval technology used in the Civil War. The website below goes into more detail on the war's battles at sea. How is the information from the website the same as the information in Chapter Four? What new information did you learn from the website?

NAVAL ACTIONS OF THE CIVIL WAR
abdocorelibrary.com/civil-war-tech

SUPPORT SYSTEMS

Weapons are the most visible technological tools in warfare. But advanced weapons are not enough to win a war. Behind the scenes, support technology helps armies communicate. It lets them spot approaching enemies. It allows them to transport troops and equipment. All these factors can give a commander the upper hand in battle.

THE TELEGRAPH

The telegraph changed communication. In previous wars, sending orders to troops was a lengthy process. Messengers would ride

Operators of mobile telegraphs could send messages to distant military commanders.

UP AND AWAY FROM THE FIGHT

Balloons provided a bird's eye view of Civil War battles. Baskets for passengers were suspended below these large balloons. Soldiers in the balloons could get a better idea of what was happening on the ground. President Lincoln even established an official Balloon Corps for this purpose. Some balloon operators sent information in telegraph messages through wires strung down to the ground. The Union made much more use of balloon technology than the Confederacy did.

on horseback. After a battle began, leaders had to wait a long time for reports from the field. Once they received these reports, the leaders could finally adjust their plans.

The telegraph made it possible for Lincoln to talk to his generals much more quickly. The telegraph was invented by Samuel Morse in 1844. It carried messages many miles over cables almost instantly. Mobile telegraph wagons communicated to and from the front lines. The Union made heavy use of the technology. But the Confederacy made little progress in this field.

Telegraph wagons strung their own lines as they moved with the army.

CALCIUM FLOODLIGHTS

Union engineers found a solution to one of the biggest problems soldiers faced at night. They could not see their targets well in the dark. Staging a nighttime attack was difficult. To solve this problem, the engineers

UNION AND CONFEDERATE INDUSTRY

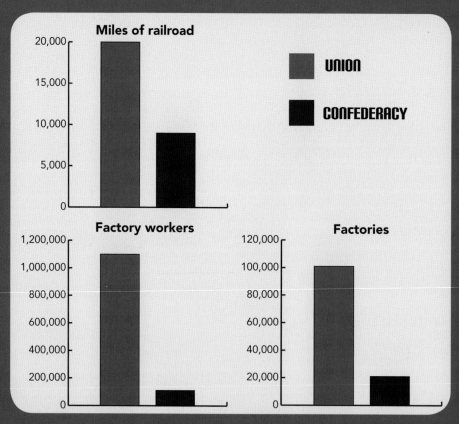

Miles of railroad

UNION

CONFEDERACY

Factory workers

Factories

These graphs compare the industrial power of the Union and the Confederacy. How might each of these factors have played a role in the conflict? How does technology affect each factor?

turned to a solution that lighthouses had been using since the 1830s.

Chemical lamps called calcium lights could illuminate enemy territory. Made from calcium oxide, these lights also offered an advantage in battle. The blinding lights made it harder for the enemy to see. The lights also proved helpful for spotting enemy ships.

THE RAILROAD

Railroads made a huge difference during the Civil War. Trains moved soldiers and supplies to the front lines more quickly than in previous wars. They also moved heavy artillery weapons from one location to another.

PERSPECTIVES
PHOTOGRAPHY

The stories of previous wars had been told through paintings, drawings, and writings. The Civil War was recorded in photographs. The process of taking pictures then was hard. The first photographs were produced using glass plates and chemicals. Photographers such as Mathew Brady captured the bloody aftermath of brutal battles. One newspaper noted, "Mr. Brady has done something to bring home to us the terrible reality and earnestness of war. If he has not brought bodies and laid them in our dooryards and along the streets, he has done something very like it."

The South had about 9,000 miles (14,484 km) of track at the start of the Civil War. Its tracks were built at various widths. To go from one track to another, cargo had to be unloaded and put on a new train. The North had 20,000 miles (32,187 km) of track. The widths were standardized. The North also had better factories to build new trains.

The Union's weapons and support technology gave it a clear advantage. The war ended on April 9, 1865. On that day, Confederate general Robert E. Lee surrendered to Union general Ulysses S. Grant. The fighting was over, but the war's technology would continue to play a role in future armed conflicts.

STRAIGHT TO THE
SOURCE

Writer Thomas F. Army Jr. explains that Civil War technology was often the result of problems in need of new and imaginative solutions. He also pointed out that many of these solutions depended on the work of everyday people who supported the cause:

> The outcome of the Civil War depended on the Union army's ability to improvise and take the war to the South. Northern armies operated on unfamiliar terrain, which included mountain ranges, swamps and wetlands, alluvial plains, forests, and rugged hills, all of which were difficult to cross because of dismal road systems and poorly mapped landscapes. . . . Why was it that Grant's engineers and his infantry, turned engineers, were able to tackle these unusual problems with such ingenious solutions? The answer rests in the textile mills, railroad yards, small farms, and mechanics' shops of antebellum America.

Source: Thomas F. Army Jr. *Engineering Victory: How Technology Won the Civil War.* Baltimore, MD: Johns Hopkins University Press, 2016. Print. 12.

What's the Big Idea?
Take a close look at this passage. Why might Southern troops have held an advantage on their own territory? How did the Union use engineers to overcome this advantage?

IMPORTANT
DATES

1844
Samuel Morse invents the telegraph.

1849
Claude-Étienne Minié invents Minié bullets.

1861
Confederate soldiers capture equipment from an armory in Harpers Ferry, Virginia.

1862
President Abraham Lincoln visits West Point to observe the Parrott rifle.

1862
Richard Gatling receives a patent for his Gatling gun.

1862

On March 8, the CSS *Virginia* destroys the USS *Cumberland* and the USS *Congress*.

1862

On March 9, the CSS *Virginia* and the USS *Monito*r battle at Hampton Roads, Virginia.

1863

In November the *H. L. Hunley*, a Confederate submarine, sinks the Union's *Housatonic*.

1864–1865

The Union Army lays siege to Petersburg, Virginia.

1865

On April 9, Robert E. Lee surrenders to Ulysses S. Grant, officially ending the Civil War.

STOP AND
THINK

Dig Deeper

After reading this book, what questions do you still have about the technology used in the Civil War? Find a few reliable sources that will help you answer these questions. Write a paragraph about what you learned in this process.

Another View

This book discusses the technology used in the Civil War. As you know, every source is different. Ask an adult to help you find another source about this topic. Write a short essay comparing and contrasting the new source's point of view with that of this book's author. What is the point of view of each author?

Take a Stand

This book discusses the use of mines, at the time called torpedoes, used in the Civil War. Do you think this weapon was an example of smart technology or, as some thought at the time, a cowardly weapon? Write an essay about your opinion. Use evidence to support your answer.

Surprise Me

This book discusses military technologies that are much different from what we see today. After reading this book, what facts about Civil War technology did you find most surprising? Write a few sentences about each one. Why did you find them surprising?

GLOSSARY

alluvial plains
largely flat landforms created by sediment from rivers

antebellum
existing before the Civil War period

cavalry
horse-mounted troops

engineers
people who design machinery

patented
given the exclusive right by a government to manufacture and sell an invention

secede
to withdraw from a nation

superintendent
a person who directs or manages a school, organization, or other entity

turret
an armored, revolving gun platform on a ship

LEARN MORE

Books

The Civil War: A Visual History. London: DK Publishing, 2015.

Halls, Kelly Milner. *Life during the Civil War.* Minneapolis, MN: Abdo Publishing, 2015.

Schanzer, Rosalyn. *Abe vs. Jeff: The Civil War as Seen from Both Sides.* Washington, DC: National Geographic, 2017.

Websites

To learn more about War Technology, visit **abdobooklinks.com**. These links are routinely monitored and updated to provide the most current information available.

Visit **abdocorelibrary.com** for free additional tools for teachers and students.

INDEX

About the Author

Tammy Gagne has written dozens of books for both adults and children. Her recent titles include *Incredible Military Weapons* and *Military Dogs*. She lives in northern New England with her husband, son, and pets.